The World of
Baby Animals

by
Ton van Eerbeek

BALL**OO**N B**OO**KS™

ORANGUTAN

What does the name 'orangutan' mean?

* It is an Indonesian word that means 'person of the forest.'

This young orangutan lives together with its mother and father in the forests of Indonesia. Its long arms allow it to swing from branch to branch where it looks for fruits and leaves to eat.

CHIMPANZEE

A young chimpanzee
always stays close to its mother.
Sometimes they walk hand in hand.
Chimpanzees share feelings similar
to humans. For instance, they comfort one another by
hugging and kissing. They are also very intelligent.

Did you know that some chimpanzees have been taught to communicate through sign language?

MACAQUE

Do you know another name for macaques?

* Snow monkeys.

Two young macaques
huddle together because they're cold.
They live in Japan with their family.
During the winter, they seek out hot springs
where they stay to keep themselves warm.

HORSE

A baby horse is called a foal.
About an hour after it's born,
a foal is able to stand to nurse
from its mother. Soon after, its legs become
strong enough to gallop. Horses and humans share
a special relationship as partners and friends.

*A boy foal is called a colt.
What do you call
a girl foal?*

A filly.

DONKEY

The Spanish word for donkey is ...

* burro.

Donkeys, unlike horses, make a funny "heee-haaaw" sound. They do this because they can make sounds both as they inhale and as they exhale. Grown up donkeys usually do work such as carry people and pull carts. Donkeys belong to the horse family.

GOAT

Goats have
a very kind and playful nature.
They are curious about everything
around them. They often live on farms as pets or to provide
milk, which is made into cheese. Goats eat grass and other
plants. In the winter, they eat hay.

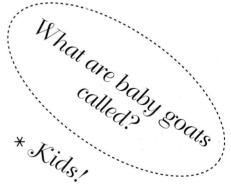

What are baby goats called?

* Kids!

How many breeds are recognized by the American Kennel Club?

* 147.

DOG

Baby dogs are called puppies. At birth, they are blind, deaf, and unable to walk. At three to four weeks old, they start to hear and walk around. Then they become playful, wrestling with one another and climbing on their mother's back.

CAT

A baby cat is called
a kitten. Kittens are able
to open their eyes about nine
days after they are born. When they're
little, they nurse from their mother. By three months,
they're able to hunt for food, such as mice and birds.

In America, a black cat is thought to bring bad luck. But did you know that in England, black cats are thought to bring good luck?

COW

Cows give us lots of milk. Do you know how much?

* In its lifetime, a cow can give 200,000 glasses of milk!

A baby cow is called a calf. In the first few months of life, a calf drinks milk from its mother's udder so that it can grow big and strong. Once a calf is grown up, it weighs about 1400 pounds.

SHEEP

A newborn sheep is called a lamb. Most lambs are born in the spring. A mother sheep normally gives birth to two lambs. Lambs stay with their mother until they are five months old. At six months, they are considered full grown.

How many different kinds of sheep do you think there are in the world?

* 914!

In the photo, you can see the pattern on the giraffe's coat. Did you know that no two patterns are the same?

GIRAFFE

Mother giraffes give birth standing up. For the babies, that means falling nine feet to the ground. Miraculously, they don't get hurt! Their long necks let them nurse from their tall mothers, and their long legs allow them to run away from predators.

DEER

A baby deer is called
a fawn. A baby deer's white
markings allow it to hide in
the tall grass when danger threatens. There are
about 30 different species of deer, ranging from
a height of 12 inches to over six feet!

Never touch a baby deer! Its mother might reject it if she smells humans.

SEA LION

Male sea lions can weigh up to 600 pounds!

Sea lions belong to the seal family. The babies are called pups. Sea lions can live on land and in water. They use their four flippers to move about. They mostly eat fish, squid, and octopus.

HARP SEAL

* When they're fully grown a harp-shaped pattern appears on their backs and sides.

Why are they called harp seals?

Baby harp seals are born on ice drifts or on snowy beaches in the North American and European arctic. They're born with yellowish fur, which turns white after a few days. The white fur lets them hide in the snow so hungry polar bears can't find them.

How loud do you think a lion roars?

* He roars so loudly that it can be heard by people up to 6 miles away!

LION

"The lion is the king of the jungle", so the saying goes. That's because this very strong African predator doesn't have natural enemies. Lions live in groups called "prides" ranging from 4 to 37 members.

TIGER

The tiger comes
from Asian forests. Adult tigers
live alone, except for mother tigers
with babies. Such a group is called
a "streak". Baby tigers, called cubs,
nurse from their mothers but later hunt their own prey.

Can a tiger swim?
* Yes, they can swim and, unlike all other cats, they actually enjoy getting wet!

PUMA

Do you know another name for pumas?

* They are also known as cougars and mountain lions.

Pumas live in North America. A mother puma will give birth to two, three, or four cubs. As adults, pumas are the champion jumpers among cats. A puma can jump 30 feet across and 18 feet straight up a cliff!

CHEETAH

* A cheetah has "tear lines" running from its eyes along both sides of its nose.

How can you distinguish the cheetah from the leopard?

Cheetahs are unique cats. They dislike water so much that they take dust baths! What's more, they are the only cats that can't retract their claws. A cheetah can stand as still as a statue. If it senses danger, a cheetah can freeze position for up to 20 minutes.

FOX

Foxes live in holes, deep in the ground with many entrances and exits. A mother fox is called a "vixen", and her babies are called "cubs", "pups", or "kits". They are born hairless but soon grow a black coat, which then turns sandy.

What do you call the hole in which baby foxes are born?

* It is called a den.

WILD BOAR

Mother boars can have three litters a year, usually with three to eight piglets in each litter. That's more than any other mammal in North America. During a boar's first year, it looks like it's wearing striped pajamas—that's its camouflage.

What is a wild boar's nest made of?

* It is made of sticks and grass.

What's special about the squirrel's sight?

* A squirrel can see above, below, and behind itself without moving its head.

SQUIRREL

A mother squirrel builds a nest high in a tree to give birth to her babies. Baby squirrels are about the size of your pinkie finger when they're born and weigh 8 to 12 grams, about as much as two quarters. After four weeks, they open their eyes.

AFRICAN ELEPHANT

A baby elephant grows
inside its mother for 22 months.
A newborn elephant weighs about
250 pounds. However, it will have to grow
for 15 years until it reaches its mother's weight
of 4000 pounds.

How much does an elephant's tusk weigh?
*A tusk weighs about nine pounds!

Index